We, the Teachers

We, the Teachers

Terry Herndon on Education and Democracy

Terry E Herndon

Seven Locks Press

Cabin John, Md./Washington, D.C.

Library of Congress Cataloging in Publication Data

Herndon, Terry
We, the teachers

  Includes bibliographical references and index.

  1. Public schools—United States—Addresses, essays, lectures. 2.
Educational equalization—United States—Addresses, essays,
lectures. 3. Collective bargaining—Teachers—United States—
Addresses, essays, lectures. 4. Education and state—United States—
Addresses, essays, lectures. 5. Peace—Study and teaching—Ad-
dresses, essays, lectures. I. Title.
LA212.H47 1983   379.73   83-8597
ISBN 0-932020-20-8
ISBN 0-932020-21-6 (pbk.)

Manufactured in the United States of America

Designed by Chuck Myers

Typography and composition by Composition Systems Inc.

Arlington, Virginia

Printed by the Maple Press Company, York, Pennsylvania

First edition, September 1983

SEVEN LOCKS PRESS

Publishers
P.O. Box 72
Cabin John, Maryland 20818

Seven Locks Press is an affiliate of Calvin Kytle Associates

Dedication

THE PUBLIC SCHOOLS have a variety of critics. Some are well intended; some are colleagues in the cause to enhance the system. Others are mean spirited and destructive. Each has equal right to speak.

During the past decade the latter have become both louder and meaner. Moreover, they have won political victories that make them more powerful.

Nevertheless, the public school teachers have struggled. They endure the demoralizing attacks and survive the paltry pay. They go to school, work hard, and teach with compassion and dedication. They have become the moderators of a political system that is negligent, and too often hostile, in its response to the young. More than ever they are the mediators between our youth and our adult society.

This book is dedicated to these teachers. It is dedicated, as well, to my wife and daughters—in appreciation for the important part they have played in my work with and for the public school teachers.

Foreword

by W. Averell Harriman

THROUGHOUT MY LIFE, I have been grateful
for America's democracy. Consequently, I
have always appreciated the value of America's public schools, for the two are inextricably and profoundly intertwined.

Since the emergence of our nation in the
eighteenth century, the education of all
Americans has been a keystone of our democracy. Over the generations, it has been
acclaimed that the truest path to participatory government is through an enlightened
citizenry. It has devolved upon our public
schools to develop this citizenry.

This burden has proved to be a staggering
responsibility, yet it has been borne with
amazing success. The United States has the
world's highest literacy rate, the highest per-
centage of high school and college graduates, and an unparalleled record of scholas-
tic, scientific, military, social, and economic
success. We have accomplished more than
any other society in the history of the world.

America's public schools have always been

a source of our nation's pride. Yet, these same schools often have been a target of public criticism.

This paradox is both lamentable and understandable. Because our public schools are public, they belong to everyone. They are supported and financed by everyone. They must, therefore, respond to the vastly divergent needs and aspirations of a vastly divergent intellectual, political, ethnic, and economic constituency. In attempting to be everything to everyone, the schools sometimes fail. Our public educational institutions are expected to provide equal educational opportunity for all and excellence in all the components—college preparation, vocational training, math, science, social studies, driver education, sex education, sports, and all the other disciplines. Is this realistic? I think not. Yet, we expect it.

From time to time, great leaders in and outside of education have addressed these and similar issues. Each brings a different perspective to the debate, and each contributes to the shaping of this country's public policies. Mr. Herndon has joined this debate with alacrity, intelligence, understanding, compassion, commitment, and tough-mindedness.

Foreword

I know of no organization that has helped shape the destiny of public education more than the National Education Association since its inception in 1857. As fresh evidence, I submit this book, which is a compilation of excerpts from speeches Mr. Herndon gave as NEA's executive director over the last tumultuous decade. It offers some of his insights into topics such as education, teaching, politics, government, national security, world affairs, human and civil rights, and democracy. It is a personal and profound examination of the ins and outs of public education in America—great accomplishment on the one hand and incessant criticism on the other.

I believe you will find these insights to be penetrating and erudite. Most of all, you will find them, as I did, to be immensely helpful in understanding the joys and frustrations of a public school teacher. It is, perhaps, as a public school advocate that Mr. Herndon's light shines the brightest. He reaches out from his classroom experience and forces us to examine our public schools from a perspective that we too often overlook or ignore.

Mr. Herndon's qualities as a human being also leap from these pages. I know him as an astute, aggressive, and compassionate leader. It is my hope that the reader will share my interest in him and also appreciate his values. I recommend his book as a primer to understand better our public schools and the people who teach in them.

Contents

Introduction

IN MAY, 1973 Terry Herndon became the executive director of the National Education Association. He was only 34 at the time, yet he had already made his mark in education. A dedicated biology and English teacher, he had become an articulate advocate, first for his local education association and later for the Michigan Education Association. He had become a skilled organizer and negotiator. His political acumen was widely respected.

As NEA's executive director, Terry was to need all these talents.

The years between 1973 and 1983—his decade as NEA's top staffer—saw America's public schools repeatedly strained and tested. Enrollments fell and budgets tightened. Political opportunists translated taxpayer frustration into meat-axe tax cuts at the same time schools were taking on new responsibilities to better educate the disabled and non-English-speaking students. Desegregation sputtered and stalled. Recession and record unemployment ended a quarter-century of prosperity. Critics—serious and cavalier—questioned and attacked public school performance. RIF (Reduction in Force) became the new ABC of teacher job security. Low salaries drove highly qualified professionals out of education altogether.

Throughout the world of education, these upsetting events produced hand-wringing galore. There was consternation. There was hysteria. And then there was Terry, through it all a true teacher who always understood our schools' basic obligations to our students —and our democracy.

I served as an officer of the National Education Association through most of Terry's tenure. Over our years as colleagues, I had the pleasure of hearing him speak hundreds of times, in every forum imaginable—from the classrooms of the smallest central schools to the nation's largest convention halls. For me, and I think for many other men and women who have dedicated their careers to educating young people, Terry gave voice to the hopes and frustrations, the perils and delights of what it means to be a teacher today.

The pages that follow place many of his words before you. They also place before you a man who, like all true teachers, has never stopped learning and growing.

May we all learn from his example.

—Willard McGuire
President, National Education
Association
April 1983

We, the Teachers

1

<u>On Society and Schooling</u>

*"Buffer for an adult world that
often fears its own children."*

L IFE AS IT IS COMES TO SCHOOL each
day. It is the school's reality. The challenge to educate, to socialize, to develop,
and to help is there as it appears — not as
it is hoped for — each day. There is no alternative for teachers but to accept the
challenge. Reinforced with the financial,
political, and moral support of the community, it is an exciting and rewarding
challenge. Without reinforcement it is
mind-boggling. (1975)[1]

THE MAJORITY of today's school children are from homes where both parents, or the only parent, work during the day. One study suggests that typical middle-class fathers spend an average of thirty-eight seconds a day in intimate interaction with their year-old infants. About two million children are battered and two hundred thousand are killed each year, mostly in their homes. Twenty million American children live with an alcoholic parent. No wonder that the typical American preschooler spends fifty hours a week watching TV.

The family is thus, increasingly, joining the list of institutions that cannot fulfill their traditional roles in the lives of youth. Nevertheless, the children as they are — with unfilled needs, hopes, and aspirations — come to school. For a growing number of these children, the school — not by consent or decision, but by default — is the only institution providing planned and orderly socialization.

The instruments through which the school performs this singular role — the adults who provide the support, discipline and the care to pull it off — are the teachers. Not only do teachers stand increasingly isolated with this enormous responsibility, but the youth population is far more difficult, and probably more self-destructive, than any that has gone before.

More than one million youths run away each year. Professor Urie Bronfenbrenner cites FBI data showing that arrests of children under eighteen for murder, assault, rape, and robbery have gone up 200 percent in fifteen years; arrests for lesser crimes are up 200 percent; arrests for trafficking and using drugs, up 4,600 percent. Fully one of each nine American young people will be arrested and in court before the age of eighteen. The suicide rate for fifteen to nineteen year-olds has tripled in less than twenty years. Two of every three deaths in the five-to-eighteen-year-old group are the result of violence.

So I say to the reporters, the columnists, the editors, the politicians, and the school bureaucrats who grumble about test scores and public-school costs as

though time stood still, "Go to school."
The school of 1977 is not the school of
1957 or 1947. It is not the school you went
to. It is not the school you remember.

(1977)[2]

WE ARE NOW in a situation where there is no way that schools can make everybody happy. In altogether too many communities we can't even make the majority happy.

Public expectations are schizophrenic. On the one hand we have a group of citizens who believe that the purpose of the school is to facilitate the process of social change, who argue that the school ought to respond in a sensitive way to the fact that we are not a monolithic society — all white, all privileged, all Anglo-Saxon in origin and Protestant in conviction. On the other hand, we have a group of citizens who say, "Hey, wait a minute, the purpose of the schools, which *we* created, is to sustain our social order, not to change it. Schools should help perpetuate the traditional values of this community." Although in most communities none of these groups appears to be an overwhelming majority, each is often large enough to grind the process of schooling to a halt.

We have a schizophrenic government, too. On the one hand, judges and the judicial system strike down restrictions on free speech. But what do the politicians say? The politicians insist that teachers tame the reckless, deal forcefully with obscenity, and squelch the seditious: "If teachers can't or won't do this, they are not functioning properly." So say the people who vote the money.

Judges proclaim that students possess meaningful rights that cannot be abridged, expanding education to the point of a proprietary right that cannot be withdrawn without some semblance of due process. But what do the politicians say? They speak of stern discipline and the need to run the unruly out of our schools. If teachers don't purge the schools, they say, teachers are not doing their jobs. The courts mandate that a minimal sense of justice demands desegregation, integration, and busing. But the politicians say there will not be any busing. They play legal and legislative games to make sure there are no monies available to finance court orders.

Other moral, legal and political storms have combined to create a situation where seventh-grade addiction, eighth-grade pregnancy, and ninth-grade convictions are commonplace. Meanwhile, all too many bureaucrats — with no recognition of the social setting in which teachers are forced to teach — babble about accountability. (1975)[3]

AMONG THE PEOPLE SERVED by our public schools, more than twenty million households have experienced a loss of job, layoff, or reduction in work hours during the past year. Thirteen million households — nearly one in five — have had someone out of work.

Our economic malaise is now long-standing. It has seriously disrupted the lives and hopes of millions, and its spectre has frightened millions more.

So we have a majority in this country with deeply felt economic and political fears, people, who seeing no credible leaders with a plausible basis for hope, continue their own, largely defensive, strategies for the protection of their way of life.

We also have a sizeable minority, with similar needs and more grievous problems, demanding a change in their way of life.

In this environment we run schools.

(1975)[1]

THE CHILDREN are not immune to the neuroses of the society at large. Insecurity, like peace, can be induced if not directly transmitted. To understand today's school we must understand this insecurity.

Many don't try. Many can close their eyes and send their children to school. But the teacher who receives these children cannot merely dream of simpler times — when all saw and embraced the virtue of hard work, the primacy and sanctity of the family, the nobility of the American tradition.

The teacher must deal meaningfully with a student who sees no correlation between effort and achievement; who sees no reconciliation between "government by the people, of the people, and for the people" and our present forms of government, and who regularly witnesses addiction, pregnancy, and assaults among peers.   (1975)[1]

TEACHERS are doing a tough, frustrating, and often times lonely job. We are a buffer for an adult world that often fears its own children.

Yet we are not unappreciated. When asked, 65 percent of the sample children told Daniel Yankelovich that they liked their teacher a lot. When asked to whom they would go for help in dealing with a troubled child, 49 percent of the sample parents responded, "the teacher"; clergymen and psychologists were a distant second and third. That, my friends, is affirmation.

But appreciation for individual performances is not enough. Appreciation of the individual teacher contributes little to relieving the adversities, correcting the inequities, or conquering the inadequacies that have resulted from the political neglect of our schools' reality. Last year, at least 13 school districts closed because they simply ran out of money. (1977)[2]

2

On Today's Teacher

"No longer the collectively employed domestic servant."

I N 1857 James Buchanan was struggling through the first year of his presidency. Workers were laying the great cable across the floor of the Atlantic Ocean. Native Americans were being trammeled by the Europeans' headlong rush to inhabit North America from coast to coast. The U.S. Supreme Court decided that Dred Scott was property. Slaves were selling for $700 each on the Richmond market, but in Texas the price had spiraled to $1,900 each, with a healthy seven-year-old male bringing $840. Drums signaling armed conflict between the states were beating with an increasingly ominous cadence, and *Uncle*

Tom's Cabin was adding dangerous sparks to the impending conflagration.

As a result of the California gold rush several years earlier, the nation was in the throes of a great depression. Over 6,000 businesses had collapsed; 8,200 banks had closed their doors; many of the prosperous had lost their fortunes, and millions of workers had lost their jobs. Unruly crowds and hunger marches were daily occurrences, and the U.S. Marines were called out to protect the banks and customhouses. Teachers were earning less than $1,000 per year. School conditions ranged from spartan to wretched.

It was against this troubled mosaic that forty-two educators gathered in Philadelphia, Pennsylvania in August, 1857 to found the National Teachers Association, the direct predecessor of the National Education Association.

It proved to be a watershed event in the history of American education. Predictably, the delegates' speeches and conversations centered on the economy, the evolving public schools, student discipline, teachers' salaries, human rights, and the threat of war. At the second meeting one year later, Horace Mann exhorted those in attendance to pursue two objectives fundamental to professional development. "First," he said, "secure as much money as you possibly can for your teaching position. Second, do the best job you possibly can of educating your students."

The record will show that the teachers present at NEA's birth were concerned about the human condition, the poor, the disadvantaged, and the many in desperate need of a quality education. In the 125 years since then, dynamic changes have occurred within the teaching profession, but NEA's egalitarian principles have held constant.   (1980)[5]

REMEMBER "Our Miss Brooks?" She was a dandy. Or "Mr. Peepers?" He was a lovely character, too. The two of them had something in common besides their success as television characters. That something made up the teacher's public image in the 1950s.

Our Miss Brooks and Mr. Peepers tended to be a bit obsequious. They were subservient. They were almost helpless. They were relatively uninformed. They had a nonaggression pact with the world. They didn't bother anybody, and they hoped that nobody would bother them. They did not participate in any significant civic or public activity. They spent most of their time trying to work themselves out of holes they had dug for themselves.

Miss Brooks and Mr. Peepers were never typical of America's school teachers. Still, in the public mind they formed the teacher's collective image, and it is an image that persists today despite the fact that today's teachers are vastly different from their counterparts of the fifties. (1977)[6]

HISTORICALLY, American teachers have been collectively employed domestic servants. They were employed as an extension of the family. Their role in life was to perpetuate traditional values in the younger generation and to house break kids so they would be equipped to carry out the traditions of their forebears.

Teachers are no longer content to play this role. We choose to look at our tradition more objectively. We choose that which is good and reject that which is bad, because it is obvious to any who are enlightened that the American tradition has not been entirely good. Much of our tradition was rooted in racism, sexism, ethnocentrism, and destructive forms of nationalism. Today the American school teacher fights to improve the social order, believing that tomorrow's world can be a different world, a better world. Many of us were active leaders in the civil-rights movement, the student-rights movement, the free-speech movement, and the anti-war movement that characterized campuses during the last decade.

Virtually all of today's teachers are college graduates, and the majority hold at least a master's degree. We are as well educated as the administrators in the schools and better educated than most board members. We're self-confident, mature, independent, and capable. We are no longer quite as poverty-stricken as we once were. To be sure, we have not made the economic progress that we would like to make or that we intend to make, but we are no longer community-owned. We participate in the flow of economic activity as consumers and frequently, if there are two teachers in the family, as investors. We now have the economic ability to participate in the political system, and we're participating with greater and greater effect.

Not only have we changed our collective personality, we have organized. Teachers have no intuitive, inherent capacity for organization. Each of us has been through sixteen, eighteen, nineteen years of formal education with people telling us to stand by our individual consciences, to value individualism, and not to compromise our convictions.

We have been obliged to come together as a matter of enlightened self-interest. Once we decided that we wanted to make a difference in the world, we quickly learned that we had no authority to make the changes needed; that authority was vested elsewhere. Somehow, we had to find the power to make people who had the authority behave as they ought to behave.

So we organized. (1977)[6]

Terry Herndon

IN THE PAST, teachers' leaders were appointed by school superintendents. Not any more. Today's leaders are chosen by other teachers. Today's leaders are pragmatic. They're hard-nosed. They're conflict-oriented, and they welcome the conflict. They understand that the maintenance of their power and influence is contingent upon delivering the bacon for the teachers who chose them. That's a profound change in the structure of our profession.   (1975)[4]

A N NEA survey shows that while a majority of Americans believe the quality of education to be as good or better than when they went to school, 45 percent believe that the quality of education has declined. That's a dramatic change from 1973, when a Gallup poll found that 61 percent thought it better and only 20 percent considered it worse. It's hard not to take the criticism personally. But it is important that we distinguish between local and national perspectives. For example, only 8 percent of the national sample had complaints about their own community schools. In fact, three in four believe their own schools to be as good as or better than those elsewhere. Yet 45 percent of the respondents believe that the quality of education in the country as a whole is worse today than when they went to school.

This we/they distinction also permeates most opinion surveys on a number of noneducation issues. This points to a dissatisfaction based on assumptions rather than personal experience. The key point is this: *There is little expressed dis-*

enchantment with local schools. The perception of declining quality comes into play only when the public comments on the national scene. Knowing this helps us understand the frequent inconsistency between what we experience at the local level and what we read about the national level. (1978)[7]

A MISSIONARY in Africa was strongly interested in teaching survival skills to the people, but he got overruled by his bishop who felt it was important that he teach them reading, writing, and arithmetic. So the missionary set about teaching them reading, writing, and arithmetic, and the children all became very proficient in all three. A couple of years later the bishop came by for a visit and found there weren't any people left. "What happened to the village?" he asked. The missionary explained that while the people were sitting around reading, writing, and arithmetizing, the lions came and ate them up.

I do not quarrel with the importance of reading, writing, and arithmetic, and I don't think the back-to-the-basics people are all wrong. I think they're wrong only when they set the three Rs apart from the fundamental social skills necessary to survive with sanity in a complex, technological society.   (1978)[8]

Terry Herndon

CONTRAST TRADITIONAL CLASS-ROOMS with which most of us are familiar with those in the "new era." In the old we find a teacher and twenty-five to thirty students. The teacher has been trained to *translate* the school's curriculum so that it makes sense for the students, *plan* an instructional program, *execute* that program using a wide variety of activities and materials, and *evaluate* the results. Most significantly, the kind of professional preparation that produced these skills was based on working with a limited range of students with abilities skewed to a high average.

In today's classroom there may still be twenty-five or thirty-five students, but among them now will be former drop-outs, push-outs, and left-outs. The handicapped are only the most recent additions: now we have the deaf, the orthopedically impaired youngster, *and/or* the youngster with visual handicaps. Some teachers will have only one handicapped student; others will have more.

Picture, if you will, how the teaching of reading, writing and arithmetic will now take place. How will map-reading skills be taught to the blind? Perhaps more importantly, how will teachers go about helping non-handicapped students learn compassion, understanding, and respect for differences?

There are, of course, effective ways to help handicapped students learn and techniques for cultivating mutually beneficial relationships between normal children and exceptional children. The problem is that teachers who have no personal experience to call on must be taught what these techniques are, how to use them, and how to adapt them for use in their classrooms.

There is a "Catch 22" provision in Public Law 94-142 (Education for the Handicapped) that makes the teacher retraining problem very difficult. Training can be paid for out of 94-142 funds but not until after the handicapped students are in the classroom. It is as if we gave a doctor specialized training only after the patient arrived.

Typical in-service education is not going to solve the problems brought about by the implementation of 94-142. Most colleges and universities are not equipped to help the practicing teacher do a better job working in these new situations. The best teacher retraining will most likely occur when we tap the ideas of teachers themselves. Teachers learn best from each other.   (1978)[9]

WE NEED MORE teacher involvement in general policy making. I don't mean involvement in curriculum decisions, but general policies articulated by school boards: the shape, texture, and color of buildings; the fashioning of playgrounds; the nature of school parks and where they are located. In other words, the decisions about how the learning experience is organized. We are entitled to a partnership in this arena.

When it comes to pedagogical decisions — how one goes about teaching and how one deals with the children in the classroom — I believe teachers should thoroughly dominate such decisions; others should stand back and play the role of teacher-helper. This includes supportive professors in colleges and universities. It includes researchers, whether they be in the National Institute of Education or at a university. It includes superintendents, principals, assistant principals, counselors, state superintendents of public instruction; it includes organization staff, like myself. It includes the people in the state departments of education; it includes the planners. All these people have one purpose in life. It is their job to help teachers do the job where the tires hit the road — in the classroom.   (1977)[6]

COMMENTATORS SUGGEST that school costs have gone up while their results have stayed the same. Not so. By default, the decision was made some years ago that the schools were going to run the largest juvenile delinquency program in town, but nobody said, "Here's another million dollars to do that." When it was decided, that the schools should run the largest drug therapy program in town, nobody said, "Here's more money for that." This society once held that parents were to deliver their children to school; now the system brings them to school. We feed them if they don't get fed at home. We take care of their psychological disorders. We take care of the sociological displacements. To the extent we are able, we take care of whatever therapeutic needs they have. Nobody has ever said, "We're going to add another responsibility to the school, and here's the money to do it."

Furthermore, we are beginning to approach universal education for five to eighteen year olds. We have a higher proportion of the five-to-eighteen-year-old population in school than ever in our history. There already exist programs for children under five. Now the Congress has mandated education for the handicapped.

Nobody talks about these changes. We need to. (1977)[6]

AVERAGES SUGGEST that we have made substantial progress over the past decade in reducing the number of students that the average teacher teaches. There is, however, no such thing as a national perspective. Each one of our teachers inherits a real classroom; effective mainstreaming is probably obstructed if the number of students in that classroom exceeds twenty or twenty-one. It is no consolation to a teacher in Manhattan or a teacher in Philadelphia or, for that matter, a teacher in rural Mississippi with thirty-eight to forty students to know that national averages are looking good or that somewhere in the United States there is a classroom — probably taught by one of America's better-paid teachers, probably attended by America's more affluent students — with only eighteen students. There is no such thing as an average teacher. (1978)[9]

IMPERSONAL administrative arrangements — with rules, schedules, arrangements, and power flowing down from the top — breed subordination and dependency. Invariably, such a mechanism spawns systems of rewards for conformity rather than creativity. Such systems induce compliance with institutional expectations rather than response to client needs. Most unfortunately, they set the stage for conflict between administrative authority and professional judgment, or between the institutional representatives (teachers) and the institution's patrons (students and parents).

Such systems are, to be sure, tidy and efficient. For this reason they are the order of the day in our schools. Accordingly, teachers are denied the excitement of formulating their own programs and then accounting to their peers and patrons for the results. Even the most competent are reduced to the routine performance of specified tasks in specified ways at specified times in specified stations. (1975)[4]

3

On Learning and Teaching

*"Most people
have never contemplated the complexity
of teaching."*

I AM PERSUADED that most people have never contemplated the complexity of teaching. For most this is understandable. Throughout their lives they learn. That which is learned has meaning and that which is not learned does not. It's different for a teacher. That which a student does not learn represents a failure, a frustrated objective of value and meaning. It is more than a momentary frustration.

I was once a high-school biology student. My teacher gave me a microscope, some modest instruction in focusing and slidemaking, and an assignment: I was to observe and sketch the cell structure of an onion skin. A whole new world opened. I saw a cell for the first time. I saw cell structure, starch crystals, osmosis, and selective staining. From that moment, I wanted to learn everything I could about cells, tissues, biochemical reactions, permeability, diffusion, food storage, light refraction, and microtechniques. I moved on to become a biology major at Wayne State University, a graduate student majoring in biology and education, and, ultimately, a certified biology teacher.

Early in my teaching career, I gave my students microscopes, some modest instruction in focusing and slide-making, and an assignment: They were to observe and sketch the cell structure of an onion skin. A few did so and had the same joy of discovery that I had experienced. Some performed the task but did so with relative indifference. Some tried and failed. Some copied the sketches of friends. Still others headed for the text to find an illustration to be copied.

Never before that moment had I considered that onion skin cells were not intrinsically interesting. Neither had I realized that some children simply cannot see through a microscope. Furthermore, I had not considered that, in this mode of presentation, the cognition sought might be precluded by technical and/or perceptual incapacity. Neither professor nor supervisor had ever raised these possibilities and their consequent pedagogical trade-offs. My confrontation with reality was personal and lonely. I backed up and started again.   (1980)[10]

Terry Herndon

IS THERE a positive or a negative connection between the muscle development required to write without strenuous effort and the intellectual development required to conceptualize a significant treatise? Are grammatical skills and rhetorical skills normally related, or are they independent of each other? These are profound pedagogical questions. I am a licensed teacher and I don't know the answers.

Is there an observable, measurable developmental trait that correlates with a child's ability to appreciate chronology or is there a normal age at which chronology becomes understandable? I don't know but I should; and the answer seems important to the teaching of history of any kind.

Have you thought about the difference between editing a paper and teaching somebody to write? Both exercises involve correcting papers, but one seeks a better paper and the other a writer capable of writing a better paper without the help of the editor. Teaching somebody to write requires evaluation of all possible explanations for errors, isolation of the real causes, and the definition of an appropriate plan for remedial development. I was licensed to teach English, but nobody ever talked to me about these differences.

I wanted to teach. I jumped the hoops. I was granted a master's degree and a license to teach. I was employed. I taught. I learned, and I was reasonably successful with most children. I was not, however, taught to teach by the college of education. Neither was I given a significant foundation of science about teaching. This is wrong.

I claim that teacher education has not well served the profession, aspiring teachers, or education. There is obvious negative fallout for the profession in that the certificate to teach is not necessarily a seal of competence to teach, as it should be. Accordingly, the license lacks the value it ought to have.

Further, much that is wrong in teacher education results not from lack of effort by those in the field but from the parsimonious attitude of the political system toward teacher education and teachers. The faculties in our schools of education are generally overworked, underpaid, and poorly organized. Very little economic or academic respect is bestowed on their research, their scholarship, or their teaching. Absent reversal in the parsimony, discussion of reform in teacher education will have little effect on the schools. (1980)[10]

A S THINGS ARE, individual teachers are generally left to evolve a personal and pragmatic approach to the practice of teaching. They have no clear professional authority or scientific rationale. George Denemark of the University of Kentucky well describes the resultant condition as one in which the teacher's rationale is usually that "it works for me." Given a proper professional education, we should be able to cite concrete scientific authority for our hypotheses and decisions or well-documented clinical experiences as the bases for our expectations. In sum, I share Denemark's view that "a major task of teacher education is that of elevating the level of teaching practice from the personal to the professional through the expansion and utilization of research, professional wisdom, and logical analysis."   (1980)[10]

I THINK it possible to profile the academic requirements of the teacher's tasks and to identify the skills, knowledge, and insights that a realistic, job-related teacher education program would provide. Such as:

• General awareness of the recognized fields of academic endeavor that make up the whole school program and a high-level expertise in the disciplines to be taught.

• *Bona fide* expertise in developmental psychology with particular emphasis on cognitive development, learning, and motivation.

• Comprehensive working knowledge of psychometrics and diagnostic procedures.

• Competence in research methods, statistics, and observational techniques, with a focus on applications to the behavioral sciences.

• *Bona fide* expertise in sociology and cultural anthropology, with focus on the relationships between culture and personal behavior.

• Awareness of the political and legal

history of education in America and the contemporary political and legal environment for education.

• Comprehensive awareness of the historical and contemporary literature on pedagogy and expertise regarding the premises and experiences of significant schools of pedagogical thought.

• Thorough competence in the use of oral and written language.

• Mastery of pedagogical techniques pertinent to the discipline to be taught.

Moreover, the program should include practical studies in such areas as human relations, group dynamics, and instructional technology. It should be integrated with or followed by a very task-specific, clinical internship that bridges the gap between theory and practice through the prudent and creative application of science to the real and highly variable world of teaching. This internship must, of necessity, entail a higher order of responsibility in the college of education than is extant at the moment. It must be viewed as an integral part of the teacher education program, and the college should be obligated to provide intensive on-site instruction, supervision, assistance, and evaluation. The end point should be the presentation and defense of an experience-based thesis, leading to an appropriate graduate degree and a license to teach.

We would have, then, a newly licensed aspiring teacher who has demonstrated excellence in the achievement of a baccalaureate degree; completed a rigorous graduate-level, multi-discipline professional school program; and satisfied the requirements of a rigorous internship. Such an effort would probably require five to seven years out of the lives of our most talented young people. Anyone who believes that we will find significant numbers willing to endure this sacrifice for the promise of a position with an initial salary of $10,000 to $14,000 a year is, in my opinion, absolutely mad. The economics of the profession must change as rapidly as does teacher education or the entire development effort is doomed.

(1980)[10]

WHEN WILLIAM PENN left home in 1682, he wrote a letter to his wife and said, "For our children's learning be liberal. Spare no cost; for by such parsimony all is lost that is saved. . . ."

During the course of our founding Constitutional Convention, Thomas Jefferson, then in Paris, wrote to delegate James Madison: "Above all things, I hope the education of the common people will be attended to. . . ."

In 1785, even before the ratification of the Constitution, the Congress enacted the Ordinance for the Northwest Territory and set aside one section of land in each township for the support of schools. This was followed, in 1787, by the Ordinance for the Government of the Territory Lying Northwest of Ohio, which proclaimed government support in rather unequivocal terms: ". . .knowledge being necessary to good government and the happiness of mankind, schools and the means of education shall forever be encouraged."

The papers of Benjamin Franklin, John Adams, James Madison, James

Monroe, John Jay, Thomas Jefferson, and George Washington are assiduous regarding education and the future of the republic. When the War Between the States was over, Robert E. Lee surveyed the enormous damage and wrote: "So great have educational interests been disturbed at the South, and so much does its future condition depend upon the rising generation, that I consider the proper education of its youth one of the most important objects now to be attained, and one from which the greatest benefits may be expected."

The string of true believers can be tracked to this very day. Dwight Eisenhower, John Kennedy, Martin Luther King, and Jimmy Carter all proclaimed unbounded commitments to the schools. Even Richard Nixon and Gerald Ford slipped earnest testimonials into their veto messages.

But wait. The essence of a school is a teacher working with children; and, that being so, there can be no real commitment to schools apart from substantive commitment to teachers.

I turn to today's *Washington Post,* and I read that one of our local school boards is considering recission of a negotiated 10 percent raise as the means for balancing the budget. I turn to the want ads. There, as I can almost any day, I find advertised the following opportunities and salaries: bookkeeper, $14,000 and $15,000; accountant, $22,000 and $28,000; controller, $30,000 and $35,000; legal secretary, $18,000; clerk-typist, $16,000; alarm installer, $27,000; auto mechanic, $20,000, cocktail waitress, $18,000; Chinese cook (one year experience), $12,500.

For your information, the beginning salaries for teachers in the Washington metropolitan area (one of the nation's richest) are $11,003, Montgomery County; $11,442, Prince George's County; $11,041, Fairfax County; and $13,347, the District of Columbia. (1980)[11]

Terry Herndon

SHORTLY AFTER my first daughter was born, my father said, "You know, Terry, I've never bothered you a great deal about what you ought to do. I've tried to help you and encourage you to do what you want to do, but now that you have a family and you have increased responsibilities, don't you think you ought to go out and try to get a good job?" In 1964 I was at the bargaining table with the school board in one of the most progressive school districts in Michigan. I made a proposal, and the response from a lady board member was, "I've always respected teachers. I've always felt that teachers ought to be paid, but do you realize what you're asking for is almost as much as my husband earns?" Well, comments like these are now historic. They're *passé* because teachers will no longer apologize for their own aspirations and their own economic self-interest.

(1975)[4]

IN COLONIAL DAYS whenever a bunch of folk got together and decided they'd like to have a school for their children, they went down to the boat and bought a teacher, an indentured servant. As time went by, schools evolved into a corporate enterprise. What at one time was relatively benevolent paternalism became a good deal more indifferent and more anonymous. So, to protect and advance themselves, teachers organized. But even today teachers have not staked out their jurisdiction in the decision-making process. What does a teacher control today? Very little more than how he or she will behave. Teachers have had nothing to say about their own level of preparedness. They come into a classroom: they have nothing to say about its structure, its design, its size. They're given books; they had nothing to say about their selection and their nature. They are given a collection of students: they've had nothing to say about the number, type, or disposition. They're told to perform according to certain objectives or expectations whose formulation they had nothing to do with. They inherit a situation in which only one variable is subject to their control. That's how they cope with it.

All this is going to change. Teachers are more aware of their own deficiencies than any of their critics. They are more painfully aware of the deficiencies of their schools than any of the distant students of public education. They are demanding, and they will ultimately gain, jurisdiction over the procedures of teaching, jurisdiction over the materials utilized in teaching, jurisdiction over the allocation of resources to the instructional process. They will have jurisdiction over questions like, "How many students can be in a class designed to achieve this particular outcome?" "What types of students should be aggregated together for specific instructional purposes?"

These decisions ought to be made by the individual teacher in his or her individual relationships with individual students. The reporters who write of NEA's wish to take over public education are inaccurate. What NEA is talking about is a teacher takeover of public education.

NEA doesn't talk so much about a powerful organization as it does an organization of powerful people, of individuals with a significant jurisdiction — not only over their own behavior but over the environment in which they work. We're talking about decisions being made by the people with the most meaningful experience about the nature of the change required. (1975)[4]

Terry Herndon

TRADITIONALLY, colleges of education have been dominated by an administrative perspective. Most faculty members are former school administrators. Now I don't demean the administrative function, but it's a different perspective from that of one who has spent his or her life in the process of teaching and working with children. The researchers in education are dealing with administrative patterns. They are dealing with questions that the practitioners in education aren't asking; and, by and large, the questions that practitioners are asking go unanswered. Now it is my view that the research function, no less than the school management function, has to be geared to the experience of the practitioner. There is no point — no economic point, no social point, no professional point — to answering questions that nobody is asking. Practicing teachers have problems. They are not as well trained as they would like to be. They are not as comprehensively educated as they would like to be. They don't know as much as they would like to know about the diagnosis of learning problems, about the prescription of remedies for these learning problems, because the universities haven't learned enough about how people learn and how one can best intervene in the learning process to assure that learning occurs. These are the questions they want answered — not questions about statewide assessment, not questions about elaborate accountability programs, not questions about management by objectives, not questions about all the things that I have to deal with every day as the administrator of a big institution. I respect the administrative function, and I know that these questions are important to someone. But they are not important to teachers.

(1975)[4]

WHEN WILL WE get to the point where the experience in the classroom generates the questions to be researched? Only when the whole matter is subject to the jurisdiction of the people who have the problems, the teachers in the classroom. I believe this will happen. Why? For one thing, because teachers no longer accept professors who retreated from the reality of the classroom to the haven of the administrative office, only to come back and preach to the teachers about what teachers don't know.

Nor are teachers going to continue to respect and accept monolithic systems, whether these systems emanate from the state department of public instruction or from the major universities or from the U.S. Office of Education. There is no right answer to American education if it is imposed from on high by a single mind that believes it knows what is best for all of the people. That is antithetic to our very concept of humane, pluralistic education. Teachers are not going to tolerate elaborate programs of assessment that end up revealing only what was already known while the secrets of the instructional process continue under the dark mantle of ignorance. They are not going to stand by unprotesting while the National Institute of Education, the U.S. Office of Education, and the state departments of education squander resources in their preoccupation with management systems to such an extent that the instructional process gets no meaningful support. (1975)[4]

THE YOUNG PEOPLE I talk with persuade me that they are more competent and more comprehensively educated than any other generation in United States history. They have had exposure to facts and reality that no generation before them has ever been exposed to. DNA, lasers, chip technology, rockets, geodesic domes, terrorism, apartheid — these are now the subjects of playground conversation.

Increasing numbers of juniors taking preliminary SATs pass them and are entered into college. As a result they don't take the test as seniors. The very brightest of America's high-school graduates pass as juniors and aren't in those samples being described when the declining scores of seniors are being discussed and deplored. The whole testing issue is a bum issue.

(1977)[6]

IN 1975, in East Whittier, California, for the first time anywhere, standardized testing became the central issue in a confrontation between teachers and school managers.

A standardized test is any test that compares performance to predetermined norms and is administered in identical form to large numbers of students. College board tests are one example. Achievement tests given to elementary and secondary school children are another. So are graduate record exams. And the so-called IQ tests.

In East Whittier it was a district achievement test that the teachers objected to. In their experience the test was too rigid, it had never been validated against another test, it did not tell them what specific questions their pupils missed, and it did not give them any real help in evaluating a child's progress. Moreover, the test was routinely given not at a time convenient to the pupils but at the convenience of a shared-time computer. Not long before, the test had been given during a record heat wave, simply because the computer was ready even though the children were not.

The 300 teachers in East Whittier didn't want to give the test anymore. When the school board refused to negotiate the issue in good faith, they struck.

(1975)[12]

THE INTERPRETATION of tests is usually based on several fallacious assumptions about education. For example, to say that a skill can be tested implies that it can be explicitly defined and measured with simple means. "Surely," people say, "it's not that complex. It should be easy to find out whether a student can read or not."

Easy? If a five year old knows the alphabet and a dozen words, can she read? If a sixteen year old can fill out a driver's license application but still sounds out each word in a second-grade reader, can he read?

In Michigan, after *extensive* review, the state board of education finally managed to define reading in the broadest sense. To do this required articulation of twenty-three separate factors or objectives. To describe math skills they needed forty-five separate objectives.   (1975)[12]

STANDARDIZED TESTS take it for granted that everybody places value on whatever skill is being tested. This just isn't the case. For some parents the goal is job preparation. For some it is acceptance by a college. For some it is simply custodial care. For still others it is social adjustment or family appreciation. For the handicapped it may be coping but for the prodigy, creative writing. Since there is in fact no agreement on goals, how can there possibly be a measurement of their attainment? We also object to standardized testing because it encourages conformity at the expense of creativity. In a system geared to the norm, the only child to benefit is the absolutely average child, one who does not deviate in any way from the test makers' assumptions. Bright kids receive less attention from the teacher than the less bright. Why knock yourself out with the students who already know the answers if your job hangs on getting the slow ones over a test? Artistic children suffer, too, because the teacher must concentrate on the tested skills if the teacher wants to appear successful. In effect, the test makers are saying that creativity isn't important because it can't be tested.

The only child who probably does all right is the one with no positive or negative deviations from the assumptions of the test maker. The question is, by what right — under whose authority — do test buyers impose the test makers' definition of an absolutely normal child? Do we really want to see our daughters and sons — each a little special — pressed into compliance with a common denominator? Consider the implications. Do you realize that it is the impersonal test that dictates what your child must learn? That the test obligates a teacher to concentrate on certain subjects at the risk of his or her job? That tests written in a New Jersey testing factory may predetermine the behavior of your child's teacher? It's worth thinking about.   (1975)[12]

4

On Equity

"The essence of our democracy."

THE RECOGNITION that all are equally endowed with the right to life, liberty, and the pursuit of happiness is a necessary precondition to the survival of the system that is America.

This, more than any other reality, caused Washington, Jefferson, Adams, and the other creators of this government to fill their writings with persistent exhortations to attend to the education of all of the people. It is eminently clear that this democracy does not work and is seriously jeopardized if all of the people are not afforded equal access to the knowledge and skills required to participate in the system. Those inadequately educated to make political presentations of their interests in the struggle, those precluded by birth from participation in the economic competition, and those denied the educational keys that give access to our traditions, our culture, and our opportunities are not blessed by our democracy. They are victims, available for exploitation by alien ideologies.

The maintenance of high-quality free public schools for all who will use them is not an altruistic fancy. In America, it is an absolutely practical imperative. It has preserved democracy for us, and it is the only means to preserve democracy for our posterity. (1982)[13]

IN 1852, Frederick Douglas rose to speak: "The Fourth of July is yours, not mine. You may rejoice, I must mourn."

A scant ten and a half years later, President Lincoln signed the Emancipation Proclamation. The Proclamation was less than a full-throated cry for freedom, dignity, and equity. It was, nevertheless, an act of sublime political courage, a monumental step forward, and a source of new hope.

Douglas rose again: "It [the Proclamation] recognizes and declares the real nature of the contest and places the North on the side of justice and civilization. . . . Unquestionably the first of January, 1863, is to be the most memorable day in American annals. The Fourth of July was great, but the first of January . . . is incomparably greater. The one had respect to the mere political birth of a Nation; the last concerns the national life and character and is to determine whether that life and character shall be radiantly glorious with all high and noble virtues or infamously blackened forevermore."

More than a hundred years later, it is still to be determined whether the national life and character will be "glorious with high and noble virtues." We still live with the pernicious evil of racism.

(1981)[14]

IN 1954 the Supreme Court of the United States declared that it was illegal, indeed un-American, to maintain separate schools for black and white children. The decision in *Brown v. Board of Education,* like the Emancipation Proclamation, testified to an inglorious past and embraced a hopeful future. The hope has been violated.

Recent data affirm that with respect to segregation it's "business as usual." Nearly 40 percent of America's black children study in virtually all black schools, and nearly 70 percent attend predominantly black schools.

In 1967 the National Advisory Commission on Civil Disorders studied the causes for the insurrections and riots that were then besieging American cities.

"The problems of this society," the Commission concluded, "will not be solved unless and until our children are brought into a common encounter and encouraged to forge a new and more viable design for life."

Still we have not desegregated our schools. (1981)[14]

WHY HAVE WE not desegregated our schools? The reason, I think, is clear. It is the reactionary, cowardly pandering to popular fears.

Consider if you will:

1. Congressman Marvin Esch amended the Education Amendments of 1974 to prohibit any federal agency from ordering a desegregation plan requiring transportation of students beyond the school next closest to their homes.

2. Senator Robert Byrd amended the HEW Appropriations Act of 1975 and 1976 to forbid the use of funds for the transportation of any student other than the one nearest home.

3. Senators Eagleton and Biden amended the HEW Appropriations Act of 1978 and subsequent Education Appropriations so that transportation beyond a neighborhood school can no longer be required.

4. The Congress has never provided the Department of Justice with the

funds to follow up on Education's referrals to it.

5. Secretary Bell now says that the Department of Education will stop making the referrals to Justice.

6. Congressman Collins amended the FY 81 appropriation to Justice so as to greatly restrict its ability to remediate segregation. (President Carter's veto of this bill was at least a pyrrhic victory for equity.)

7. The President of the United States advocates tuition tax credits to facilitate the further stratification and polarization of our people, and simultaneously proposes funding reductions that can decimate the capacity of our common schools to integrate the historically disadvantaged into the educational mainstream.

8. A teacher who leads a strike that closes school for a few days goes to jail and/or pays confiscatory fines, but a school board member who leads massive resistance to segrega-

tion does so with impunity or, at worst, is elected to Congress.

This list could go on and on — because in a country where nearly half of 42 million children are transported to school, a mere 3 percent are transported for the purpose of desegregation.

The essence of our democracy is the compromise between majority rule and individual rights. Our early leaders precluded tyranny by the majority when they authorized the judiciary to protect constitutional rights from a rampant legislative majority. Throughout the seventies our "blacklashing" Congress has repudiated and circumscribed this principle; in so doing, it strikes at the essence of our national character.   (1981)[14]

Terry Herndon

S USAN B. ANTHONY, addressing the NEA convention in 1881, pointedly described every teacher's interest in the women's movement:

> "Do you not see that as long as society says that a woman is incompetent to be a lawyer, a minister or a doctor; but has ample ability to be a teacher, every male who chooses the teaching profession acknowledges that he has no more brains than a woman?"

Lest Ms. Anthony be misunderstood, I lay the point bare: We male teachers have no more brains than a sister in the profession and she has no more brains than we do. But a society that demeans women and the work of women demeans itself and every member of that society.

(1980)[5]

On Equity

HITLER'S GERMANY was not the work of a random maniac imposing his will on a people. It was a mass movement that emerged from a highly cultured and highly educated population. It always amazes me that our own highly educated population has so little cognizance of this. To a distressing degree we seem to have little comprehension of the fact that if we allow our government to set males against females, or whites against blacks, or English-speaking citizens against Spanish-speaking citizens, or the middle class against the poor, or immigrant Americans against native Americans, this same government will ultimately deny rights and benefits to us all. The white, male, English-speaking, American-born school teacher who does not understand the relationship between these pieces does not understand the teachings of history. (1981)[15]

5

On Bargaining

*"Spurn a moderate and
create a militant."*

IN WEST TEXAS they tell a story about
an old teamster crossing the country-
side with his grandson. Along the way he
snapped his bullwhip and knocked a fly
right out of the air. A little farther on, he
lashed out again and picked off a butterfly, right out of the air. The little boy's
mouth flew wide open. He had never
seen such a manifestation of power. He
thought his grandfather was really something. They went on a little further and
came to one of the few trees out in West
Texas. There was a hornets' nest hang-
ing from a low limb. The little boy said,
"Grandpa, I bet you could knock down
that hornets' nest." Grandpa was, of

course, wise with years. He stroked his beard and said, "Son, I think we better not do that. That fly was all right, and the butterfly was something, but those hornets are organized." (1977)[6]

Terry Herndon

MORE THAN their counterparts in private, commercial, and production enterprises, public workers face their clients daily and directly. Since we personally take the rap for failure, we put a high price on quality. We also, therefore, demand the optimal opportunity to succeed. Professional unions carry these concerns for quality to the bargaining table; traditional trade unions never have. In the industrial model, product quality is properly management's responsibility, not the union's. Professional employees, on the contrary, not only care about the product, but they are willing, if need be, to strike for the right to succeed.

This, believe me, is what is at the heart of teacher unrest in this country. Our membership surveys say that the number one issue for teachers is not salary but class size, and the reason teachers are most concerned about class size is that their own experience leads them to believe that it is the ratio of teacher to pupil that has most to do with the quality of education. We recently polled our membership, asking members to identify the most important changes they'd like to make in their jobs. Lower class size was at the top of the list, followed by better curricula, better administration, and, only then, higher salary.   (1975)[12]

ACROSS THE COUNTRY today there are about thirty states with some kind of statute that recognizes the bargaining process between teachers and their managers. This means that twenty states have nothing. This is not totally accurate, because some of these twenty states have statutes that make it illegal for a school board to bargain. Now, of the thirty with statutes, about fifteen authorize some variation of what I call "collective begging," for what they permit is a far cry from what I understand collective bargaining to be. Only a handful of states have set up a process that provides a reasonable alternative to what ultimately takes place in all too many states; school boards are required to talk to teachers only until they get tired of talking, at which point the teachers can either take it or leave it — with no recourse except to strike and go to jail. In many states, the process can get very complicated. For example, if the board won't talk, you can go to court and force it to the table. Or, if a board doesn't meet with you often enough, you can have it found guilty of an unfair labor practice. If you can't get anywhere, you can bring in a mediator. And if that doesn't produce anything, you can bring in a fact-finder. But in the last analysis, after jumping every recalcitrant hurdle, and after the fact-finder's report is rejected by the board, you can then either accept the board's offer or go on strike and on to jail. I don't find this a very satisfactory alternative to impasse.

In spite of all this, there is ample evidence that collective bargaining works. NEA has about 5,000 locals involved in some form of bargaining. We had 160 strikes this year. The newspapers talk and talk and talk about teacher strikes, but I haven't seen an article yet about the 4,850 negotiations each year that were successful and peaceful. In most cases the process works, but when the process does not work, the present statutory inequities under the law leave teachers standing virtually naked.   (1975)[16]

Terry Herndon

I DO NOT UNDERSTAND the justice of a system that tolerates the kind of disparity and hypocrisy that we find in federal policy. Forty years ago the Wagner Act became the law of the land. If one studies the history of the law and reads the preamble, one finds that Congress decided as follows: one, the public has a vital interest in the continuity and stability of economic enterprise; two, strikes disrupt the economy; three, the public cannot afford to have strikes. Since the public cannot afford to have strikes, workers must have the right to organize, protected by law. They must have the right to designate their bargaining agent, protected by law; and they must have the right to engage in concerted activities, including strikes, protected by law. All of this to help the process and prevent strikes.

But what does Congress say to teachers? They tell us that the public has an even greater interest in the stability of the operation of public services than it has in the private economy; and because of this, the public is injured even more when there is a strike in the public sector; and since the public is so grievously injured by a strike, remedies in the private sector designed and mandated to avert strikes shall not be available to those who work in the public sector. It is an absolutely absurd position, but it is the present policy of the United States.

If we were to achieve a federal collective bargaining law of the kind NEA has sought for years, and if we had the protections of the National Labor Relations Act, frustrated teachers would not go to jail, and school boards would not be seeking injunctions instead of settlements. I have been involved in more than one episode where a school board went to court seeking an injunction three or four days before a contract expired. Their case with the judge was, "Your Honor, you enjoin those teachers from striking. We think they're going to strike when the contract runs out, and we haven't reached agreement." It never occurred to them that the thing to do was to reach agreement. It never occurred to them because it was far easier to go to court and get an injunction. Management access to the courts in the absence of statutory equity and protection obfuscates the whole collective bargaining process and renders our people impotent.

The absence of a fair public policy established by Congress always makes our disputes with school boards moral rather than political or economic. It brings about a situation where some of our colleagues are in jails rather than in classrooms. It produces a teaching faculty that is discouraged, discontented, and often demoralized.

I don't understand this. We talk to Congressmen and they tell us we're right, but they do nothing. In election years they always come to us to solicit money and political support. We tell them about our problems, and they agree; they get indignant and say something ought to be done — will be done. And they still do nothing. I don't understand. I never will. (1975)[16]

On Bargaining

I T IS THE ABSENCE of bargaining rights that brings strikes and disorder. Not too long ago private-sector workers had no legally protected means to gain equity in their relationship with their employers. As a result, strikes caused widespread disruption of our productive capacity. To diminish this disruption, on the assumption that equity and stability were inseparable, in 1935 Congress passed the Wagner Act. The assumption has proven to be so demonstrably valid that we now have compatible labor codes in nearly every state. No responsible voice has advocated repeal of those codes for a couple of decades. Yet we deny these realities in the public sector. Public workers are told instead that collective bargaining fosters strikes. This is pure rubbish.

Discontent and long festering grievances do indeed contribute to unionization and strikes. It is, however, no less true that collective bargaining, mediation, factfinding, and arbitration have the potential to resolve the discontent without a strike. Equity and stability are permanently and inseparably related.

(1977)[17]

On Bargaining

THE CONSEQUENCES of state-by-state collective bargaining regulation are both illogical and inequitable. In Pennsylvania, for example, teacher strikes are entirely legal. A few miles east in New Jersey, when our members go on strike they risk arrest, jailing, and fines. What's more, in the absence of protective laws, our members are often subjected to treatment commonly accorded criminals. Last fall in Shelton, Connecticut, seven striking teachers — four of them women — were arrested, searched, deloused, and put in prison with convicted felons.

Since 1972 NEA representatives have gone before Congressional committees three times to testify on behalf of bills that could bring a new stability to the public sector. None of the bills has made it out of committee. And, in the sixth consecutive anti-public employee ruling of its term, the U.S. Supreme Court, in effect, denied Congress the power to enact our proposal. The specific case, *National League of Cities v. Usery*, had to do with whether Congress had authority to extend minimum wage and overtime provisions to state and local government employees. By a margin of five-to-four, the Court said that it did not.

Not insignificantly, the majority ruling was written by Justice William Rehnquist, the last Nixon appointee to the Court. To Justice Brennan, whose minority opinion received scant media attention, the decision was disturbingly reminiscent of those made in the 1930s by a Court that was known as the Nine Old Men and that, in its hell-bent efforts to undo the New Deal, precipitated a constitutional crisis. "I cannot recall," Justice Brennan wrote, "another instance in the Court's history when the reasoning of so many decisions covering so long a span of time has been discarded so roughshod."

It should be noted, too, that with monumental disregard for judicial consistency, the Rehnquist ruling left untouched an earlier decision upholding the federal power to freeze the wages of state and local government employees. We are, therefore, left with a Court view of constitutional equity that permits the federal government to take away wage increases but prohibits it from setting even a minimum standard for granting them.

(1977)[17]

Terry Herndon

I N A CAREER-ORIENTED, capitalistic, consumer society, one's self-concept, sense of worth, life style, social standing, and personal influence are all a function of job and earning capacity. This is no less true for fifteen million public employees than for the eighty million private-sector wage earners. There is no economic or moral theory that will cause public employees to want less than they see all around them or to perceive their jobs differently than others.

What then of increasing unionization and militancy among public employees? It's simple. Spurn a moderate and create a militant. The price of stability is equity. Deny equity and induce instability.

(1977)[17]

On Bargaining

THERE ARE two things I can say with certainty about teachers' strikes. One, teachers don't want them. Teachers will go on strike only as a last resort, only if they see no reasonable or logical alternative. Two, strikes generally reflect the morass of inequitable or ill-conceived statutes, broken promises, massive layoffs, threats of budget cuts, and the general insecurity that have beset the teaching profession. These circumstances are forcing more and more teachers to take the last resort. (1977)[17]

Terry Herndon

TO PLACE exclusive and sole blame on public employee organizations for public-sector strikes, one must hold that the public's managers (politicians) are incapable of injustice, duplicity, selfishness, insensitivity or error in judgment; or, in the alternative, one must hold that public employees should stoically endure the full weight of any injustice, duplicity, selfishness or insensitivity intentionally or mistakenly imposed on them. My respect for politicians is relatively high. Even so, I cannot accept the notion that politicians are categorically as "pure as the driven snow" or even that they are purer than their counterparts in the private economy. And, if public managers are not more noble than their private sector counterparts, why is it not reasonable and equitable that their employees—public employees—have equal protection against their ignobility! Anyone who believes that a sanitation worker is entitled to justice, a teacher to fairness, and a fire fighter to safety, must grant them the means to gain and defend these entitlements. (1977)[17]

"HE WHO HAS the gold sets the rule." This is the golden rule of the capitalists. It's the basic rule that allowed the smashing of unions throughout most of our history, created the railroad riots of 1877, moved the President and the courts to smash Eugene Debs in 1894, prompted the Supreme Court to strike down minimum wage laws throughout the thirties, stimulated Chicago's "Memorial Day Massacre" in 1937, tolerated years of indifference to the law by J.P. Stevens, and sentenced hundreds of teacher unionists to jail over the past two decades. There has always existed the notion that capital is more precious than labor; capital is the basis of all production; capital is the efficient factor in production; and capital is the very purpose of production. This notion relegates labor, the mass of people not in possession of significant capital, to the indentured service of capital.

This simple and primitive economic golden rule has served to order societies since time immemorial. Nevertheless, the democratic impulse of the disenfranchised has always pressed back. This has been seen on the meadow at Runnymede in 1215, in Philadelphia's Independence Hall in 1776, in the Petrograd strikes in 1905, in our civil rights movement of the sixties, and in the birth of Poland's Solidarity in the eighties. It is always and it is everywhere.

We are a nation born of resistance to that rule; born of a declaration that government derives its power from "the consent of the governed" and that it is the "Right of the People. . .to institute such government . . . as to them shall seem most likely to effect their Safety and Happiness." In this noble proclamation we find the charter for America's labor movement. Simply put, it is to organize the people to assure the fulfillment of the promise that our government serve all of the governed and not only the possessors of "gold." It is the guarantee that the basic elements of our society — government, commerce, and surplus production known as capital — are harnessed to provide for the "Safety

and Happiness" of our 220 million people, most of whom are labor.   (1982)[18]

6

On Politics and Politicians

*"Leadership is one thing,
officeholding another."*

W E HAVE bipartisan government and
there is ample work to be done in
each party. I do not suggest that NEA
become a politically partisan organization, but rather that our partisanship
continue on behalf of education. Our
members and leaders must, accordingly,
become more bipartisan and less non-
partisan. I ask for more work and less
rhetoric. I seek the meaningful involvement of teachers — a caring, sensitive,
informed, and creative body of teachers
— in the partisan political process that
makes our government go.   (1974)[19]

THE MOST visible expression of NEA's new character is the vigorous participation of its members in politics. But the decision to become politically involved did not come easily nor without extraordinary debate within the association. Many preferred, those first anxious days, to look the other way when the time came for politicking and contributing and volunteering. Gradually, however, our membership grew to recognize that virtually every public action affecting our profession and our students is political in nature, that our destiny as an association is inextricably tied to the quality and character and talent of those we choose to govern us.   (1979)[20]

AMERICA's teachers want the federal government to assume its fair share of financing the cost of public education, so that no child in this nation is deprived of a decent education because he or she is unlucky enough to live in a tax-poor location. America's teachers want federal legislation guaranteeing the right to organize and bargain collectively.

America's teachers want an end to the possibility of federal legislation that might merge Social Security with state or local area retirement systems to the detriment of teachers and other public workers.

America's teachers want meaningful health care legislation, energy legislation, environment legislation, and peace.

We have much to do. But we've learned the lesson that the best place to find a helping hand is at the end of your own arm. (1979)[20]

I N OCTOBER 1921, a petition to the President of the United States was signed and delivered. This petition, urging the creation of a federal department of education, stated, in part; "If the federal government is to perform its proper function in the promotion of education, the Department at Washington must be given such dignity and prominence as will command the respect of the public and merit the confidence of the educational forces of the country. The education leader of the nation should hold an outstanding position, with powers and responsibilities clearly defined, subordinate to no one except the President."

Signatories of that petition eighty-eight years ago included a diverse group — among them the president of the National Education Association; the president of the American Federation of Labor, Samuel Gompers; the sovereign grand commander of the Masons; the president of the Women's Christian

(Note: The National Education Association first called for a cabinet-level Department of Education in 1867.)

Temperance Union; the presidents of the Parent-Teacher Associations, the American Library Association, the American Council on Education, and the Daughters of the American Revolution.

In October 1979 this petition, and NEA's long-standing advocacy, were answered when President Jimmy Carter signed Public Law 96-88. (1979)[20]

NINETEEN EIGHTY was not the de-
mise of the progressive liberal coali-
tion. Nineteen eighty was not the dis-
assembling of the Democratic Party.
Nineteen eighty was not the emergence
of the radical right or the Christian right
or any other far right group as a perma-
nent prevailing influence in American
politics. Nineteen eighty, like every other
election, was the political interaction of a
candidate with a very specific set of political circumstances.

Nineteen eighty was a number of people expressing their fears, their anxieties and their hopes about bread on the
table, the destiny of their children and
how they can wend their way in a world
that is far too complex for them to fully
comprehend. Nineteen eighty was not
the mandate of an ideological elector-
ate.   (1981)[15]

LEADERSHIP is one thing, officehold-ing another.

Officeholding is preoccupied with survival. Leading is preoccupied with achieving.

Occupying an office is facilitated by the phenomenon of "tape-recorder" governance. Tape-recorder governance is taking a poll and then going to a meeting to tell other people what the poll told you they are saying. This is Richard Nixon-type government. Government by opinion polling means walking around with your finger in the air, seeing which way the wind is blowing, and then announcing to people which way the wind is blowing.

Leadership is joining the debate wherever the debate must be joined. It's a two-way process. Leadership involves elevating expectations, the level of courage, commitment, excitement, and enthusiasm for reordering the world a little bit. It doesn't take a leader to cast a directed vote. It takes a leader to go to a meeting, enter the debate, and have a meaningful exchange with the other people who have come to the meeting. It takes a leader to sift the observations, the prejudices, and the realities and come to a consensus view of truth that can be moved forward.

Officeholding is very attractive to the insecure; leadership is attractive only to the secure.

Officeholders are concerned mostly with the viability of ideas; leaders are more concerned with the quality of ideas.

Officeholders worry about others getting credit; leaders do not.

People who are leaders energize other people. Sometimes this stimulates conflict and causes debate. Sometimes it creates dissension and difficulty and occasionally a gastric ulcer. Officeholders usually hate all that. They prefer to manipulate groups rather than energize them. Energetic groups are more difficult to deal with.

Leaders understand that blame and credit go hand-in-hand; if you are in a position that entitles you to take credit for achievement, you are also in a position that requires you to take blame for lack of achievement. Officeholders love to take credit for the achievement, but they usually try to disassociate themselves from mistakes and failures by looking for a scapegoat.

Leadership cannot be legislated. Most often it is not delegated. Nor is leadership achieved by denying opportunities to other people. Leadership is circumstantial and it belongs to those who can wade into circumstances, with clear vision, energy, courage, and integrity, and grasp from circumstances the opportunity to achieve.   (1975)[3]

SCHOOLING cannot be sold profitably because the public schools are free. Therefore, Dr. Milton Friedman, intellectual husband of the Reagan Administration, would introduce a system of vouchers in lieu of our present system of public education, for in his opinion vouchers would create a whole new market. New sorts of schools would spring up in this market. Some would be nonprofit and some for profit.

Friedman admits that the possibility exists that some public schools would be left with the "dregs" and become even poorer than they are now. He accepts this as the price to be paid.

Unhappily, one cannot dismiss Friedman as merely our most eloquent spokesman for eighteenth-century economics, which he most certainly is. Others of perhaps less impressive academic credentials but larger popular constituencies are taking their cues from him. Gordon Drake of the Christian Crusade observes that "the NEA is promoting communist causes; our children are being indoctrinated for a new collectivist world government." And in "The Free Market Approach to Educational Reform," a pamphlet for the Center for Independent Education, Leonard Billett argues that if vouchers and a free market in education were established, "publicly provided education would become extinct."

The Billett-Drake-Friedman nexus might be discounted in other times, but this is now; and, in this time, no less a personage than the sitting President of the United States, a supporter of tax credits for tuition to private schools, proclaimed in a 1976 radio broadcast: ". . . tax credits will probably help schools more than parents. . .a school could raise tuition with the assurance that it wouldn't mean any actual increase in price to the parent."

If Billett-Drake-Friedman-Reagan have their way, the public schools will be removed as an impediment to "free market" education. (1981)[21]

OUR PRESIDENT and his Democratic and Republican supporters in the Congress tell us that while national security is the preeminent federal responsibility, there is no federal responsibility to assure, enhance, and equalize the quality of public schools. The President and his tuition tax credit allies tell us that while we cannot afford to finance our public schools, we have billions available to assist private schools.

Whether they be motivated by greed, malice or simple ignorance and confusion, they imperil the future of our democracy. They are a real and urgent threat to much more than the job security of our members, and to much more than the economic security of American citizens. They threaten the security that is the greatness of the United States.

(1982)[13]

Terry Herndon

I DON'T FEAR the foolish voice of the radical right nearly so much as I fear the spineless politician — the legislator, the congressional representative or senator, the governor, the superintendent of schools — who abandons leadership for prominence in a parade that the politician knows is going in the wrong direction. The cowardly clamor of the self-serving right is of no consequence unless those in public office abandon their responsibility and leave a leadership vacuum for the far right to fill. (1979)[22]

LOOKING to Poland, we can see that it is possible to secure a government without protecting personal liberties. In El Salvador, we see that the state can be maintained without fairness. South Africa provides evidence that a free-market economy can be sustained amid horrendous inequities and outrageous disparity of educational opportunity. We, however, are Americans, and our legacy is more than the security of the government, more than maintenance of the state, and more than the sustenance of an established economic order. Our challenge is to secure the blessings of liberty for our posterity, to maintain a government that attends to the safety and happiness of the people, and to assure that government "of the people, by the people, for the people, shall not perish from the earth."

This demands education. This demands equity. This demands fairness. This demands universal, free public schools of the highest quality producible by the best of our minds, the best of our efforts, and the first appropriation of our money. We can settle for no less.

(1982)[13]

7

On Community Control and Federal Responsibility

"Ignorance is the enemy."

FRED HECHINGER of the *New York Times* has put it succinctly: "Public education in the United States is in mortal danger." You and I know that, but it is a measure of that danger that most Americans do not. The vast majority of Americans who believe in the public schools, who in poll after poll reaffirm their pride and confidence in their local schools, understand neither the nature of our fiscal crisis nor the nature of the overloaded social problems in our classrooms that make it increasingly difficult for our children to learn and our teachers to teach. Convinced, apparently, that the news stories of school closings and teacher layoffs and declining test scores and teen-age drugs, alcohol, and violence are about schools somewhere else, they abandon the field to a noisy minority waving the banners of Proposition 13 and "Back to the Basics." Enter, then, a new breed of reactionaries.

The neo-conservative movement has escalated the average American's desire for equity and efficiency in government spending to a hysterical demand to reduce all public funding. Even worse, the movement is exploiting the average American's understandable concern that so many of our children are growing up functionally illiterate. "Back to Basics" has now become the rhetorical platform for irrational attacks not only on teachers and administrators but on the functional objectives of education — socializing, serving, producing, and discovering. These skills are fundamental to the very objectives that have traditionally defined the role of the public schools in our democracy.

This movement will not be reversed, in my judgment, until those of us who have the responsibility for running the schools and teaching the children form a united front. It will not be reversed until we look beneath and beyond the glib, simplistic, and treacherous petitions of the back-to-basics advocates and find out — by *asking* what it is citizens truly expect of the schools in the communities where they live, and tailor our curricula, our teaching methods, and our administrative systems accordingly. I'm talking about local citizen control. Real local control, not the mindless incantations of the "back-to-basics" crowd. (1979)[23]

As THINGS STAND, local control of education is fast becoming more myth than reality. Our local schools now are confronted by an array of federal and state mandates — drug education, career education, aid to handicapped children, bilingual education, economic education, metric education, to name only a few of the special programs mandated by the state and federal governments since 1970. Why all these federal mandates? In part they result from a failure of local schools to recognize and respond to local needs. Is there any serious doubt that school desegregation and affirmative action were federally legislated because we failed to meet the needs of black citizens at the local level? Is it not one of the political realities that any continuing need, pressed but unfulfilled at the local level, will in time become a national goal, encouraged and supported by the laws and regulations of the federal government?

Why this persistent failure at the local level? It is, I think, because in the messy arrangement that passes for American education policy there is a notable vacuum — the almost complete absence of *local* educational policies developed and articulated through a continuing dialogue among teachers, parents, administrators, legislators, and those taxpayers who are either childless or whose children are no longer of school age. In other words, a dialogue between the servers and those whom the schools serve. Contrary to what is being offered as conventional wisdom, our funding problems will be resolved only when we have thought through the relationship of local control to learning, and when we have set up reliable arrangements for accommodating the local curriculum to expressed community interests. There are, to my knowledge, almost no school districts in this country where local educational policies are developed and defined in terms that would meet the minimum test of participatory democracy.

(1979)[23]

IF BACK to the basics means anything at all, it should mean a return to the basic principles of American education, among them that: all students must have an equal opportunity to develop, within the limits of their abilities, the fundamental skills to handle language, numbers, and complex ideas; that such basic skills are only an essential first step toward an education; that true education must also take into account individual differences; that we should strive for excellence, not simply competence, and that, as John Gardner has so eloquently reminded us, excellence must be on a par with equal opportunity among this society's educational goals.   (1979)[23]

IN 1905 Elwood Cubberly was the authority on school finance. At that time
he decreed that educational opportunity
not be limited by the taxing ability of the
local school district. He cried for equalization of opportunity. In 1971, sixty-five
years later, the scholars who made up the
Education Finance Project reported.
They made the same finding and issued
the same call.

Yet in 1973-74 the average per-pupil
expenditure in New York was $2,037
and in Kentucky $729. The situation is
more graphic when one contemplates
that New York's $2,037 per child re-
quired the investment of 6.29 percent of
personal income while the citizens of
New Mexico invested 7.58 percent of
personal income but spent a mere $1,220
per child. Illinois and Arkansas each ap-
propriated 4.7 percent of personal income, but in Illinois this appropriation
generated $1,228 per child, while in Ar-
kansas the yield was only $773.

In spite of these inequities, we continue to require that more than 50 percent of school money come from local

taxes and more than 40 percent from the states. It is to this harshly unjust system that schools are forced to turn for fiscal capability. (1975)[4]

OUR POLITICIANS are making a serious mistake if they interpret the current mood as an unqualified opposition to government spending. NEA's survey of last year found substantial support for raising more money from local sources to improve public schools. Our polls for the past five years have registered steady support for increased federal spending on education.

Clearly, then, in any effort to increase public support for public education, the public is not to be regarded as the enemy. Inflation is the enemy. And, as always, ignorance is the enemy. Most particularly, the public is woefully uninformed about the economic foundations of local schools. Ninety percent either overestimate the amount of money provided by the federal government or have no idea at all about how school funds are raised. By and large, they have yet to see the connection between the reduction in property taxes, which they want, and a reduction in school services, which they distinctly do not want. (1979)[23]

OUR HIGHWAYS started off as footpaths. People walked through the woods, around a swamp, and between the trees. They got a horse, the path got a little wider; they got a wagon, the path got a little wider. Soon there were automobiles, and they hardtopped the path. But people still had to go around the swamp and between the trees. Then they got cars that went 120 miles an hour, so they took these little roads, cut down the trees and made six-lane superhighways. Now we can watch people whipping around the invisible swamp at 100 miles an hour.

One such town with the road around the swamp had a serious problem. The cars went off the road. People were maimed and killed there every day. The city officials decided they'd have to do something about that. So they called all the highway experts together and said, "We've got to do something. Citizens are being maimed and killed out there on that curve. Ambulances are running back and forth and rushing to the hospital." Most people thought they ought to straighten the road, but there was one fellow who won out. His suggestion was that they build a hospital right on the curve.

And that's the way it is with school finance. It's a sick joke, and to perpetuate it much longer is intolerable. It is time for Congress of the United States to accept its responsibility for a well-financed system of basic, comprehensive education for all the young people in this country. Congress has never faced this obligation. Congress has not done it because too few of us act as if we believe that Congress should do it. How many people have ever talked to their representatives in Congress about this problem? How many people have ever even suggested to members of the local school board that they ought to engage in an active program of education for their representatives in Congress? How many have demanded a positive congressional response on education funding as the bedrock condition for political support?

(1977)[6]

Terry Herndon

WE HAVE RESOLVED that quality education for all is critical to the well-being of the society. We declare that opportunity must be equally available to all races, all classes, and both sexes. We favor local control of schools but argue that the absence of controlling authority neither immunizes the Congress from a compelling responsibility nor excuses its woeful neglect of public education.

(1979)[24]

8

On Peace

*"It is nearly impossible to educate
a child to make peace on the block
while making war in the world."*

I SEE more clearly now than I ever have
that it is not possible for us to do the
job for education while ignoring the economic and policy environment in which
we try to do that job. If we do not deal
with questions such as tax and economic
policies, decent treatment for the poor,
equity for all of the people, and the
creeping militarism that is enveloping
the capacity of this country to serve and
care about people, we will lose the fight
for education and the fight for decency;
we will lose the fight for justice; we
will, in fact, lose the fight for our very
future. (1982)[25]

I AM a husband and father. I am a teacher. I am a God-fearing American. From beneath each hat I speak my woe for a government that forsakes the downtrodden and the disenfranchised and gouges the laborers to enhance the comfort of the comfortable and to fuel the most expensive war machine in the history of the world.

This government has enacted into law the largest tax cut in history and delivered extraordinary financial windfalls to wealthy individuals and powerful corporations. And now the perpetrators tell us that we cannot afford to provide proper schools for our children; higher education for graduates; safety enforcement for our workers; income assistance or job training for the unemployed; food, medicine, or legal aid for the indigent.

The Treasury Department reports that Congress has exempted major industries — automobiles, transportation, and mining — from any tax whatsoever on income from new investments; indeed, these industries will receive what

118

amounts to a tax subsidy to use against income from past investments. Meanwhile, we debate whether we can afford to sustain the Social Security system, and consider another $8-billion cut in child benefit programs. In spite of soaring interest rates that inflate the price of all goods and services, the President proposes a budget with a $90 to $100-billion deficit to finance a $1.5 trillion five-year military program and a $240 billion military budget. This is more than $1,000 per American.

This is crazy, and I must ask, "What are we becoming? What kind of a people are we?" (1982)[25]

I WANT to live. I want to live in peace. I want to live with hope. I want to secure the blessings of liberty for my posterity. Nuclear holocaust does not relate to a single one of my personal aspirations, yet I am taxed and taxed to sustain its grisly probability.

Have you ever considered that there is no record in the whole of human history of the invention of an effective weapon that was not eventually used? As you ponder that simple historical fact please consider as well that there are now 40,000 to 50,000 nuclear weapons in the world and that their explosive power exceeds one million Hiroshima bombs — four tons of TNT for every man, woman, and child alive today. Add to that the technical reality that any one of these weapons can annihilate the larger part of any major city in the world. Clearly, the explosion of a small fraction of the world's arsenal would mean that civilization as we know it will cease to be. Experts and common citizens alike see this as an increasingly probable event, yet we continue with business as usual: We set it aside to watch the Superbowl, to check our papers, to write our reports. (1982)[25]

THE BUDGET that our President has placed before the Congress of the United States is a moral outrage.

It is based on an inequitable revenue system.

It is oblivious to the needs of millions of people.

It retreats from fulfilling the fundamental purposes and promises of the nation.

It presents deficits that will impair economic development.

Even more outrageous, it commits a peace-loving people to the acceleration of a bizarre adventure in militarism as the means of national security. We are told that in 1984, like the followers of Orwell's Big Brother, we will accept the delusion that "War is Peace." It will not be so for me.

I am a teacher who sees beauty in each person.

I am a teacher striving for one family of humankind.

I am a teacher craving liberty and freedom for all people.

I am a teacher encouraging love, compassion, and understand ing between people and nations.

I am a teacher struggling to resolve hatred among people.

I am a teacher repulsed by the oppression of the body, the mind, and the spirit.

I am a teacher angered by the exploitation of the weaker among us.

I am a teacher tormented by the futility of war among my brothers and sisters who are the children of God.

I and those I love may yet be victims of the contemporary madness, but I will resist and press for peace. *I will follow no leader who does not speak honestly and reasonably of peace.* (1982)[25]

PEACE is not a matter to be consigned to military planners, strategic think tanks or wise, pin-striped men in isolated offices. It is the people's issue. They have not only the right but the responsibility to speak.

No less a soldier than President Dwight Eisenhower said, "I like to believe that people in the long run are going to do more to promote peace than are governments. Indeed, I think that people want peace so much that one of these days government had better get out of their way and let them have it." Of the peoples of the earth, it is only those of us who enjoy democracy and know liberty who can accept that challenge. It is we, and only we, who bear personal responsibility for the course of our government. (1982)[26]

I SPEND a great deal of time railing against the corporations, the corporate interests, and the profit mongers. I spend a great deal of time railing against Republican administrations and their conservative policies. But profit-greedy corporations and reactionary Republicans are not the basic problem.

Historically, we've all been on a fly-now, pay-later kind of trip. The trip is over. We've had the trip for two centuries and now the bill must be paid. We're not going back to three-dollar oil when that's the only resource available for the millions of people to uplift their status and achieve some of the conditions of living that we have enjoyed in this country for two centuries. We're not going to continue hauling bauxite out of Jamaica or copper out of South America so that we can maintain a standard of living that consumes 25 percent of the world's resources for our relatively insignificant portion of the total population — not without paying a much greater price. The rest of the world is not going to let us consume resources that are converted from raw materials to finished products by workers making $8, $10 or $12 an hour while the workers that broke their backs to gouge it out of the earth make 35 40 and 50 cents an hour. Those days are rapidly ending. There is going to be a significant redistribution of the plenty of the earth. Our tradition of exploitation, both domestically and universally, is going to come to a screeching halt.

Gandhi said that this earth is adequate to our needs but not to our greeds. I believe this to be true. The American people will have to learn the differences between their needs and their greeds, and this will cause great trauma.

The kinds of changes to come will generate profound, traumatic, and anxiety-laden social experiences. There will be, as the process of adjustment goes on— particularly if it occurs without a sense of humaneness, sensitivity, and compassion — very explosive social movements in this country; social movements demanding change, social movements resisting change, and conflicts between the two. And I'm fearful that these crosscurrents will only increase the trend toward war and international conflict unless we respect the legitimacy of the aspirations of people in other parts of the world.

I have an abiding hope that the American people can, through education, learning, sensitivity, and awareness, demand a government that articulates a public policy with a greater impact for good.

But to make this happen, teachers must be different — and schools must be different. (1975)[4]

AMERICA'S teachers are daily about the task of making society what it should be and can be. It is this which gives our work special meaning.

It is, it must be, optimistic work. It derives from faith that people can be different and, indeed, can choose to be different; and a corollary faith that societies and governments can be elevated by rational and charitable commitments. One can scarcely be satisfied in teaching unless one believes these to be true.

The work is emphatically moral and is beset by extraordinary moral responsibility. We must decide to encourage love or encourage hatred. We must choose to inspire love of life or, in the alternative, allow a sense of despair. We can elevate the spirit to hope, or we can let it atrophy.   (1982)[27]

PREPARATION for peace requires a deep and abiding devotion to life, a compelling respect for the fundamental human rights of all people, a meaningful appreciation for the differences among people, a sense of charity toward people in need, an understanding of interdependence, and the tolerance to forbear while mediation, conciliation, arbitration, litigation, and legislation move forward toward justice and equity. Indeed, it is nearly impossible to educate a child to make peace on the block while making war in the world.

The schools, then, need the powerful commitment of their community and their nation if they are to make their contribution to a better life. In this regard, the nation's flirtation with military superiority is dangerous not only because of its *per se* enhancement of the probability of war, but also because the requisite diversion of resources from development, justice, and education severely undermines our capacity to prepare for peace. The incessant conditioning of public attitude to accept the arms race is counterproductive to education for peace. Teachers are the natural enemies of war. $(1982)^{27}$

On Peace

WHEN TIMES are "hot" (for example, the unfortunate Vietnam experience), military policy and the peace-war issue are front and center. When the times are "cold," military policy becomes more theoretical and is readily subordinated to economic anxieties. The erratic nature of our concern is explainable, in part, by the relationship of our political process to such an ambiguous issue as peace. Most major political organizations are organized around an economic concern and, therefore, on economic issues are always vigorously present in the political process. Peace, however, is generally viewed as the absence of war. Therefore, in the absence of a real war or the threat of war (as provided by Carter's saber-rattling around Afghanistan, Reagan's adventure in El Salvador, or Haig's talk of a theater nuclear war in Europe), peace is taken for granted just like good health. In this phase, one sees virtually no political activism directed at sustaining the peace.

In this interval of political pacifism by the people, the political process yields to economic interests associated with armaments and to the military's preoccupation with enemies. Preparation transcends legitimacy and responds to every conceivable or hypothetical foreign threat. In other words, the debate becomes unbalanced; militarism goes unchecked.   (1982)[28]

ANY STUDENT of American politics knows that the capacity to respond to any domestic need, the capacity to divert resources to any of the many endeavors of our government, is determined more than by anything else by economic and defense policies. Because of the economic policies of the Reagan Administration, we have enacted the largest tax cut in the history of the republic. We have changed the pattern of revenue collection by our government so that that slice of the public which can afford it least must bear the heaviest burden for the support of government; and we have increased the magnitude of those burdens. This has dramatic implications for what we can do about education today; but it also has a lot to do with our potential for responding to education needs two, three, eight, and fifteen years from now. It is likewise true that as government borrows enormous sums of money to sustain a mounting deficit encouraged for the purpose of building up our military capacity, we impair the over-

all economic ability of the society to provide for other things.

Anybody who cares about education
but wanders through Washington oblivious to economic and military policy is
doing nothing productive. One cannot
talk seriously about the nation's education policy without first considering the
impact of military and economic policy
on the capacity of government to respond to the needs of schools.   (1982)[26]

OUR FIRST PRESIDENT could look across the sea to England and say to his fellow revolutionaries, "The nation which endulges toward another an habitual hatred . . . is in some degree a slave." The wisdom in Washington's words is more evident every day. Yet our government seems more responsive to the Soviet presence than to the needs of its own people.

We ring the globe with military installations because of the Soviets. We flood Europe with missiles because of the Soviets. We indulged Thieu, Lon Nol, and the Shah because of the Soviets. We shrink from confrontation with apartheid because of the Soviets. Now we are urged to open our public lands to more aggressive mineral development because the Soviets are waging a "resource war," and we are pressured to cut general welfare efforts because of the further Soviet nuclear buildup.

Neither we nor the Soviets can rely on the seas to shield us from one another. As the missile flies we are thirty minutes apart. The span diminishes with each new technical development or strategic placement of a launching device. The wonders of science have brought us to the imperative that we grudgingly respect our reciprocal destructive power. Our windows of vulnerability are opened, never to be closed. We can only learn to live with open windows.

Our response to this reality will measure the kind of people we have become and determine the kind of nation we shall be. We are poised today like the zealots of Masada preparing to destroy ourselves in the face of an awesome enemy. The difference, of course, is that, should we execute the plan, we will destroy the enemy too, and there may well be no civilization to chronicle the epic.

(1982)[26]

THE OMNIPRESENT nuclear umbrella has not created jobs, filled bellies, ended oppression, or forestalled Soviet exploitation of human misery in the Third World. Moreover, neither aggressive arms supply nor bellicose diplomacy arrested the creep of Marxism into Vietnam, Cuba, Nicaragua, El Salvador, or Afghanistan. Then why do we rely on these policies for future defense? We should, instead, at home and abroad, attend compassionately to the promotion of justice and human rights; the encouragement of economic development; the provision of food, medicine, and schools; and the preservation of peace.

It is for the people of the nation to decide whether we will be a model of freedom for the world or the anxiety of the world. The better course is tougher. It requires a solid and fair economy, a healthy, well-educated, and hopeful population, and a stable, peaceful world order. The other course is easy. It requires only arms, threats, bellicose rhetoric, and more arms. (1982)[26]

9
Afterword

THE GOAL is not mere schooling, but schooling that befits a democracy: a system of schools officially and emphatically hostile to all forms of discrimination or inequality; a system of schools officially and emphatically loyal to freedom of conscience and religion, freedom of speech, freedom of association, and freedom to criticize; a system of schools officially and emphatically dedicated to freedom of inquiry, freedom to study, freedom to propose and experiment, and freedom to teach; a system of schools officially and emphatically insulated from the pressures of economic, ecclesiastical, and militaristic orthodoxy; a system of schools officially and emphatically dedicated to universal excellence.

Such schools are essential to the reclamation of prosperity; for knowledge and inspiration are as essential to invention as is necessity.

Such schools are essential to the reconstruction of community and the sustenance of equity.

Such schools are essential to a capacity for peacemaking. Humankind will survive *only* if we find an alternative to the threat of war as the principal instrument of foreign policy. Where but through education can we hope to gain the knowledge and the insights necessary to find this alternative? (1982)[13]

Sources

1. Remarks, National Press Club, October 9, 1975.

2. Address, NEA Annual Meeting, July 4, 1977.

3. Address, "The Making of a Leader," NCSEA Presidents Leadership Conference, July 23, 1975.

4. Remarks, Alumni Education Day, Albion College, April 12, 1975.

5. Address, NEA Annual Meeting, July 5, 1980.

6. Address, Montana Delegate Assembly, April 15, 1977.

7. Address, Arizona Education Association, December 8, 1978.

8. Address, KONA Institute Day, February 17, 1978.

9. Address, "Training Teachers for a New Era," Institute for Educational Leadership, Conference on the Education of All Handicapped Children Act, April 19, 1978.

10. Address, Teacher Education Assembly, Harrisburg, Pa., 1980.

11. Address, Teacher Hall of Fame, 1980.

12. Address, Commonwealth Club, San Francisco, December 19, 1975.

13. Address, NEA Annual Meeting, July 4, 1982.

14. Address, San Francisco State University, 1981.

15. Comments, Fourth Annual Legislative Conference, NEA, 1981.

16. Remarks, Minnesota Education Association Negotiation Conference, November, 1975.

17. Address, "Equity and Stability in Public Employment," Atlanta, January, 1977.

18. Comments, Americans for Democratic Action, March 6, 1982.

19. Address, NEA Annual Meeting, 1974.

20. Remarks, "Gala Celebrating the Creation of the Department of Education," Washington, December 6, 1979.

21. Address, NEA Annual Meeting, Minneapolis, July 5, 1981.

22. Address, NEA Annual Meeting, Detroit, July 5, 1979.

23. First draft, address, "Teachers, School Boards, and the Destiny of Public Schools." National School Boards Association, April 21, 1979.

24. Final draft, address, "Teachers, School Boards, and the Destiny of Public Schools," National School Boards Association, April 21, 1979.

Sources

25. Address, Human and Civil Rights Conference, February 28, 1982.

26. Address, National Press Club, April 13, 1982.

27. Unpublished manuscript, "Education and Life," 1982.

28. Unpublished manuscript, "War and Life," 1982.

Appendix

A Citizen's Guide to Public Education Today

The Social Realities

Every year since 1975 more than one million marriages have ended in divorce.

Twenty percent of children under 18 now live in single-parent homes.

Forty percent of the children born in the 1980s will spend at least part of their lives in single-parent families.

In 1981 the ratio of childless couples to couples with children was 1.02.

More than 48 percent of mothers with children under 18 are in the labor force.

About 10,000 children are severely battered every year; 1,500 die from the battering.

In 1979 101,630 cases of child abuse were reported; 2,746 children were killed.

Sixty-eight percent of 18- to 25-year-olds have tried marijuana and/or hashish; 40 percent of 12- to 17-year-olds and almost 20 percent of those over 25 have tried these drugs.

Hallucinogens such as LSD, THC, PCP, mescaline, and peyote are used by about one in every seven students.

The highest use (more than 25 percent) of

cocaine and hallucinogens is among 18- to 25-year-olds. More than 18 percent of this age group have engaged in non-medical use of drugs legally obtainable only under a doctor's prescription.

From 1960 to 1977 arrests of children under 18 for murder, assault, rape, robbery, and aggravated assault increased 386 percent; for prostitution 687 percent; and for trafficking and using drugs 7,276 percent.

In 1979, 17.1 percent of all live births were illegitimate, 43.9 percent of which were to teen-age mothers.

Five million girls between the ages of 13 and 19, including 250,000 under age 15, are sexually active.

Every year more than one million girls between 12 and 19 become pregnant.

A total of 7,713,000 teenagers were employed in June 1977. Of these, 4,042,000 were working full time. The remainder were working part time, including 1,264,000 who claimed they had to work for economic reasons.

The Schools, 1982-83

Number of School Districts	15,885, a decline of 905 from the peak year of 1973-74
Number of buildings	86,199
Total expenditures (For current expenses, capital outlay, interest on school debt)	$116,931,093, an increase of $65,380,192 (126.9%) over 1972-73.

Cost per pupil	$2,917.00, an increase of $1,887.00 (183.2%) over 1972-73.

Expenditures by region

New England (CT, ME, MA, NH, RI, VT)	$6,540,672
Mideast (DE, DC, MD, NJ, NY, PA)	$24,872,789
Southeast (AL, AR, FL, GA, KY, LA, MS, NC, SC, TN, VA, WV)	$23,041,241
Great Lakes (IL, IN, MI, OH, WI)	$22,464,822
Plains (IO, KS, MN, MO, NE, ND, SD)	$8,693,953
Southwest (AZ, NM, OK, TX)	$11,828,635
Rocky Mountain (CO, ID, MT, UT, WY)	$3,880,505
Far West (AK, CA, HI, NV, OR)	$15,608,476

We the Teachers

Revenue

From federal
government

$8,653,277 (7.4% of
total)

From state
government

$58,445,045 (50.3%
of total)

From local
governments

$49,175,149 (42.3%
of total)

The Students

Average daily
attendance,
1982-83

36,351,396, a decrease
of 5,869,312 (13.8%)
from 1972-73.

Years in school
For every 100 pupils in 5th grade in 1972:

99 entered 9th grade in 1976
89 entered 11th grade in 1978
74 were graduated from high school in
1980
46 entered college in 1980
23 are expected to earn bachelor's
degrees in 1984

Public-School Employees, 1982-83

Total   4,000,000
Classroom teachers
  Elementary schools   1,176,711
  Secondary schools   961,861

  Total   2,138,572
  a decrease of 70,095 from 1979-80

148

Principals, supervisors, other instructional staff	288,560
Other (cafeteria employees bus drivers, maintenance people, administrative support)	1,555,684

The Teachers

	1961	1981
Median age	41	37
Sex		
Male	31.3	33.1
Female	68.7	66.9
Race		
Black	8.1	7.8
White	88.3	91.6
Other	3.6	0.7
Median years of experience	11.0	12
Highest degree held		
Less than bachelor's	14.6	0.4
Bachelor's	61.9	50.1
Master's or 6 years	23.1	49.3
Doctor's	0.4	0.3
Teachers teaching for first year	8.0	2.4
Marital Status		
Single	22.3	18.5
Married	68.0	73.0
Widowed, divorced, separated	2.2	4.8
Teachers who have children	57.9	73.6

We the Teachers

Political affiliation	*1971*	*1981*
Democrat	43.0	40.2
Republican	33.7	29.4
Other	1.5	0.4
No affiliation	21.8	30.0

Average annual salary
Elementary	$20,942
Secondary	$21,100
Total	$20,531

an increase of $10,355 over 1972-73

Salaries adjusted for inflation:

In terms of the constant 1966-67 dollar, the average classroom teacher's salary dropped from $6,821 in 1966-67 to $6,769 in 1982-83, representing a loss in purchasing power of 0.8 percent.

Teacher Supply

Beginning teachers seeking jobs in fall of 1980:   123,285

Jobs available to beginning teachers in fall of 1980:   71,425

Oversupply of beginning teachers: 51,860

On the other hand: To raise the quality of public-school education to minimum levels, 453,500 of teaching positions would have been required in fall of 1980. By this standard, U.S. was short 330,215 qualified beginning teachers.

Appendix

How Teachers Spend Their Time

- The total actual work week for teachers averages 46.1 hours; 36.3 hours are part of the required work week; 8.5 hours for noncompensated work such as grading, lesson plans, counseling; and 9.6 hours for compensated activities such as coaching sports, student newspaper, etc.
- The median class period is 55 minutes, unchanged since 1966.
- Secondary school teachers teach approximately 25 periods a week out of an average 35-period school week. Of this, 23 hours per week are spent on instruction, nine hours on other activities such as study halls, homerooms, conferences, and four hours on lesson preparation and grading.
- Teachers have an average lunch period of 35 minutes, down from 38 minutes in 1966.

Classroom Size

Nearly one-third of all secondary school teachers deal with 150 or more students a day. Nearly one-fourth of all elementary classes contain 30 or more children.

Classroom Stress

Almost 6 percent of all U.S. teachers are physically attacked by students each year; 19 percent of these require medical treatment.

About 12 percent (120,000) of all secondary

school teachers are threatened with injury by students every year.

In 1976-77 54,000 physical assaults on NEA members were reported, 5,000 more than the FBI reported as having occurred on police.

Curriculum and the Quality of Education

Expenditures for textbooks and other instructional materials have declined by 50 percent over the past 17 years.

Only eight states require high schools to offer foreign language instruction; none requires students to take the courses. Thirty-five states require only one year of mathematics; 36 require only one year of science for a diploma.

In many other industrialized nations, the time spent on mathematics, biology, chemistry, physics, and geography, based on class hours, is about three times that spent by even the most science-oriented students in U.S. schools.

In England, it is not unusual for academic high school students to spend eight hours a day at school, 220 days per year. In the United States, the typical school day lasts six hours and the school year is 180 days.

The National Education Association

Founded:	1857
National headquarters:	1201 Sixteenth St., NW Washington, DC 20036

Appendix

Total membership   1,700,000, making
it the largest
professional
association in U.S.

Of total, 85 percent are classroom teachers
Of all U.S. teachers, 69 percent belong to
NEA

Local associations and
state affiliates   12,351

Bargaining
representative for   8,500 K-12
teacher
associations
175 higher
education
faculty
organizations

Political Affairs

In 1982, of 302 NEA-endorsed candidates for
House of Representatives, 224 were elected; of
32 Senatorial candidates endorsed, 20 were
elected. In 1980, 311 delegates and 167 alternates at the Democratic National Convention
were NEA members; at the Republican National
Convention, 12 delegates and 10 alternates were
NEA members.

Note: This statistical profile of public education is
drawn from data appearing in *Marital Status & Living
Arrangements,* March 1981, U.S. Bureau of Census;
Monthly Labor Review, January 1978, U.S. Department
of Labor; *1982-83 U.S. Statistical Abstract; The Status of
the American Family,* NEA Research; *1981 Sourcebook of*

Criminal Justice Statistics; Drug Use Among American High School Students, National Institute on Drug Abuse, 1978; *Crime in the United States 1978,* Federal Bureau of Investigation; *Advance Report on Final Natality Statistics, 1979,* National Center for Health Statistics; *Teenager Sexual Activity, 1971-79,* Guttmacher Institute; *Employment & Earnings,* U.S. Bureau of Labor Statistics; *Estimates of School Statistics, 1982-83,* NEA Research; *Digest of Education Statistics,* 1982, National Center for Education Statistics; *Status of the American Public School Teacher 1980-81,* NEA Research; *Teacher Supply and Demand 1980-81,* NEA Research; *National Teacher Opinion Poll, 1979,* NEA Research; *The Safe Schools Study Report to Congress,* 1978, National Institute of Education; *A Nation at Risk,* 1983, National Commission on Excellence in Education. All data are the most recent available in April 1983.

Index

Index

Index

Index

About the Author

TERRY HERNDON was born in Russellville, Kentucky, in 1939, and moved with his parents to Detroit two years later. Educated in the public schools of Michigan, he holds B.S. and M.A. degrees from Detroit's Wayne State University. He has also studied at Albion College (Albion, Mich.), the University of Michigan at Ann Arbor, and Morehead State University (Morehead, Ky.). For five years he was a high-school teacher in Warren, Mich.

He joined the staff of the National Education Association first as a field representative in Michigan. From 1969 to 1973 he served as executive director of the Michigan Education Association. In 1973, at the age of 34, he was named NEA's executive director, serving in that capacity for the next ten years. It was during his tenure that NEA, with 1.7 million members and 12,000 local and state affiliates, emerged as a major force in American politics.

Mr. Herndon was a member of the President's Advisory Panel on Financing Elementary and Secondary Education. He shared leadership of the Peace Corps Advisory Council with Carol Bellamy, president of the New York City Council, and at various times has been president of the National Foundation for the Improvement of Education; a director of the United Nations Association; a trustee of the Council on Hemispheric Affairs and the National Planning Association; and president of Citizens Against Nuclear War. He is married to the former Mary Gandolfi and has two daughters, Holly and Julie. He and his family live in Bethesda, Md., where he is a lay minister for the Rockville Church of Christ.